Screened In Companion Workbook

A Practical, Self-Directed Guide to Living Free in the Digital Age

Anthony Silard

Cover design by Mark Eimer. Interior design by Diana Wade. Published by Inner Leadership Press.

Manufactured in the United States of America. ISBN 978-0-9817853-4-9

Published 2020.

Contents

A Guide to this Workbook   3

PART ONE: DISCONNECTED   7

1 | A History of Praising and Criticizing a New Technology   9

2 | The Bait-and-Switch of the Internet   19

3 | Social Information Versus Social Connection   27

4 | The Brogrammer Brigade   36

5 | You Are the Crash Test Dummy   45

6 | Your Digital Identity   56

7 | The Kids Are Not Alright   66

8 | Digital Drift   79

PART TWO: THE NEW WORLD ORDER   93

9 | The Meta-Democratization   94

10 | The Brand Is You   100

11 | Convenience over Enjoyment   105

12 | Your Netflix Time   116

13 | So Much Information, So Little Wisdom   124

PART THREE: RECONNECTED   133

14 | Direct Your Use of Technology, Not the Other Way Around   134

15 | Downgrade Social Media, Upgrade Your Relationships   140

16 | Digital Limiting Strategies   155

17 | The Heart of Darkness and Contain Your Phone, Expand Your Life   163

Commencement   175

How to Develop a Vision Statement and Action Plan   178

Acknowledgments   185

INNER
LEADERSHIP
PRESS

A Guide to This Workbook

Screened In Companion Workbook: A Practical, Self-Directed Guide to Living Free in the Digital Age is designed for use with Anthony Silard's *Screened In: The Art of Living Free in the Digital Age*. All quoted text can be found in the corresponding chapter of *Screened In*. This *Companion Workbook* contains sections that each correspond to the same chapter in the book. Its intended use is for:

1. **Self-Directed Individual Study**: Individuals who want to go deeper into the recommendations of *Screened In* will find a practical guide to integrate its lessons into daily life through self-reflection questions, journaling opportunities, and executable strategies designed to transform their relationship with technology. This curriculum supports individuals to go at their own pace, with the option to complete exercises chapter by chapter or after finishing the book. No matter which method is chosen, individuals who undertake the challenge of honestly analyzing their screen use and its effects will experience feelings of both happiness and freedom from their phone/devices. This *Companion Workbook* can augment the revolutionary ways *Screened In* can change lives.

2. **Group Study:** Individuals who are interested in group study will find this guide helpful in their facilitation. There are a multitude of structured challenge questions and exercises in each chapter to keep group members accountable. The note sections and journals allow members to share their thoughts as the group experiences the radical effects of the simple changes *Screened In* recommends.

3. **Classroom Study:** Teachers can join the growing number of educators who have decided to include *Screened In* as required reading to teach practical life skills, study habits, and socioemotional intelligence. The *Companion Workbook* is an essential tool for educators who want to see their students succeed in the digital age. The self-directed nature of the *Companion Workbook* is ideal for small group projects, individual assignments, and discussion group study.

4. All users, either in self-directed individual, group, or classroom study, will find this *Companion Workbook* offers:

   - Reflection questions that follow excerpts from relevant literature and passages from the book

- A **Bringing It Home: Connecting with My Goals and Values** section at the end of each chapter that provides guidance on creating personal alignment and consistency in how you approach integrating technology into your life

- Areas following each chapter to take notes on reclaiming freedom and happiness

- Digital limiting strategies and an eight-week guide to the **Heart of Darkness Challenge Journal**

- Step-by-step instruction on developing your own personal **Vision Statement** and **Action Plan**

There are seventeen chapters of the *Companion Workbook*, all corresponding to Anthony Silard's *Screened In: The Art of Living Free in the Digital Age*, a book that offers extensive peer-reviewed research, personal anecdotes, and practical strategies to better manage your relationship with your phone/devices. Consider reading a chapter each week, followed by completing the corresponding *Companion Workbook* section. Give yourself enough time to reflect on the densely packed information from the chapter and apply its lessons to your own life. When you are ready to conduct an honest assessment of your own screen use and develop strategies for improvement, sit down and begin the *Companion Workbook* questions, exercises, and journals.

1. Read the chapter of *Screened In*.

2. Go to the corresponding *Companion Workbook* section, reread any excerpts provided, and complete the challenge questions.

   Tips for individuals and group members: You are encouraged to use the *Companion Workbook* to fit your passion and interest on the subject. Please feel free to write anywhere from a few words to a few or more pages to nothing at all in response to the questions in the space provided. Alternatively, you may prefer to write pages in response to some of the questions on a separate sheet of paper, or on the extra page for notes at the end of each chapter.

3. Finish each section by completing the **Bringing It Home: Connecting with My Goals and Values** exercise. This is imperative and will be used to develop your **Vision Statement** and **Action Plan** in the final section of the *Companion Workbook*.

4. Make note of how your thoughts develop in the section **Notes on How I Will Reclaim My Freedom and Happiness in the Digital Age** at the end of each chapter.

5. Upon completion of the *Companion Workbook*, complete the **Vision Statement** and **Action Plan** in the final Commencement section.

In every way, please use the *Companion Workbook* to fit your own style of learning and journaling. Do what works for you. You may find that you tap most deeply into your creativity when you only answer a few questions at a time and then return to the *Companion Workbook* at another time. Alternatively, you may prefer to complete an entire section in one sitting. Again, it's all up to you.

The greatest challenge of this process is committing the necessary time and self-control required to make major changes in this area of your life. However, there is no time like the present: our humanness, happiness, and freedom depend on it. You are encouraged to find partners, groups, and support in this process. For additional support and more information on resources, group facilitation, and ways to get involved, please visit anthonysilard.com today.

Thank you for allowing me to be your facilitator on one of the most important journeys you can take at this stage of our collective history. I wish you well and send you positive energy in your efforts to regain your freedom and happiness in the Digital Age!

Warmly,

Tony Silard

Anthony Silard, Ph.D.

INNER
LEADERSHIP
PRESS

PART ONE:

DISCONNECTED

INNER
LEADERSHIP
PRESS

1

A History of Praising and Criticizing a New Technology

1) Consider my admission:

> *I had a sinking feeling I was unable to shake, that worsened by the minute, as I went through thousands of emails I had sent or received: they had amounted to absolutely nothing. I felt like most of my long, laborious hours spent dutifully typing away at my desktop had done nothing but raise clouds of dust.*

Describe a time when you felt this way. What strategies can you put into place to change this feeling?

2) Do you feel like your time on your phone/devices displaces valuable time with others? Describe what your time on your phone/devices displaces in your life.

3) Consider:

> Studies on the Internet's paradoxical effects abound. Take, for example, a study by cancer researchers Paula Klemm and Thomas Hardie that found that 92 percent of the participants in online cancer support groups were depressed as compared to none of the participants in face-to-face cancer support groups.
>
> Why would people living with cancer become depressed only if their group meets online? There is a displacement effect … (think: the water displaced when you drop a bowling ball in a bathtub, which I'm sure you do often) in which more time online equates to less time face-to-face with family and friends.

Write about a time when the displacement effect emerged in your life. How did it make you feel?

INNER
LEADERSHIP
PRESS

4) How does the displacement effect influence how you balance your time devoted to family or friends versus your time devoted to work?

5) What can you do to prevent the displacement effect from emerging in your life?

6) Consider:

Loneliness is not just increasing: it's skyrocketing. On both sides of the Atlantic, loneliness has become a complex, ubiquitous problem.

In the US, a Cigna survey of twenty thousand Americans released in May 2018 found that nearly half of Americans are lonely based on the UCLA Revised Loneliness Scale, a finding that has raised the decibels on siren calls of a "national loneliness epidemic." In this survey, 43 percent of Americans acknowledged that they feel isolated from others and that their relationships are sometimes or always not meaningful. Twenty-seven percent reported that they never or only rarely feel understood. A year later, Cigna conducted another survey of over 10,000 American adults and the findings—and the national trend it uncovers—are even more unsettling: over three in five Americans are now lonely.

The "epidemic" designation has also been invoked in the UK—for example, recently by the Royal College of General Practitioners— which is further ahead of the loneliness curve ever since Prime Minister Theresa May appointed a Minister for Loneliness in 2018. May made this decision on the heels of two studies that found that 9 million British citizens are often or always lonely and that British children spend less time outside than prison inmates. Yes, really.

INNER
LEADERSHIP
PRESS

Have you felt lonelier since the advent of the smartphone in 2007? If so, what have been the consequences of these feelings in your life? If not, what has buffered you from loneliness?

7) Have you observed another person in your life becoming lonelier since the advent of the smartphone? How has it affected them?

8) Describe a time when your time spent online influenced your feelings of loneliness. What was the situation? How did it make you feel?

INNER
LEADERSHIP
PRESS

9) Consider Hannah's experience:

> *After a six-year relationship ended in 2016, I jumped into another relationship in 2017. Following the most recent breakup, I realized how much I have relied on others to feel happy. I have spent the last eight years of my life relying on someone else for fulfillment. Throughout these experiences, I made it a priority to display my relationships and outings online for others to see. I wanted others to see how happy I was. Scrolling through my Instagram feed has become a bad habit and quite unhealthy because I have the tendency to compare my life with the lives of others. People have never witnessed any authenticity or my true emotion of loneliness because I choose not to upload that part of my life. I choose not to upload when I am struggling emotionally, socially, or financially. This habit has only reinforced the fact that I utilize social media as a drug to temporarily cure my social isolation.*

Does social media help alleviate your social isolation? What other means can you employ to better connect with others?

10) How do you consider the Internet to be different from its predecessors in terms of technology that "connects" us, such as the telegraph, the radio, the telephone, the automobile, and the television?

11) Why do you think the Internet has become more addictive than these earlier technologies? What addictive features does the Internet contain that these earlier technologies do not?

INNER
LEADERSHIP
PRESS

Bringing It Home: Connecting with My Goals and Values

12) What are the most important lessons you've learned in this chapter that will influence how you use your phone/devices?

13) Based on these lessons, what new goals could you commit to? (Refer back to these goals in the final section of the workbook when you develop your Action Plan.)

14) How do these new goals reflect your values? What values do you stand for and want to be remembered for that are consistent with these new goals? (Refer back to these values in the final section of the workbook when you develop your Vision Statement.)

Notes on How I Will Reclaim My Freedom and Happiness in the Digital Age

INNER
LEADERSHIP
PRESS

2

The Bait-and-Switch of the Internet

1) Has "The Bait-and-Switch of the Internet" affected your life? Describe a time when you felt "hooked" by it.

2) What challenges have you found with any "addictions" that are now technologically mediated?

3) What would be possible in your life if you were to overcome these addictions? How would you approach your personal relationships differently? How would you approach your career differently?

4) Consider the words of Stanford psychologist Kelly McGonigal: "People have a pathological relationship with their devices. People feel not just addicted, but trapped." Write about a time when you felt trapped by your device. What made you feel this way? What can you do to avoid this feeling in the future?

INNER
LEADERSHIP
PRESS

5) Consider:

> *The Internet provides a welcome respite and distraction from reality. The less comfortable we are with reality, the more appealing is an alternative. Yet it's not the Internet that is the alternative. Rather, the Internet accelerates our access to the alternative.*

Do you believe that the Internet simply enables easier access to other addictions? Alternatively, do you believe it is the Internet itself that is addictive?

6) Consider:

> *The Internet—meaning our smartphones, tablets, and laptops—accelerates the appeasement and* reduces *the social costs associated with many addictions.*

Do you agree? Why or why not? Think about your own situation. Do you have any addictions? If so, how has the Internet reduced the social costs—such as disapproval, ridicule, or being looked down upon—associated with them?

INNER
LEADERSHIP
PRESS

7) This exercise is derived from the Make It Happen exercise (in this chapter of *Screened In*):

    a) Consider what motivations and impulses cause you to log on and leave the physical world. First identify the activities that are the most alluring to you about online life. Are they Facebook and social media sites, reading the latest news (e.g., Twitter, CNN, BBC), online dating (e.g., Match, Tinder), fantasy football, gaming, email, Internet porn, discount travel, shopping (e.g., Amazon), watching unusual videos (e.g., YouTube, Facebook), reading product reviews (e.g., CNET), or repeatedly checking weather or other local conditions before going out? Whatever the activities are that draw you to your smartphone or tablet or laptop, identify them in the first column below.

Online Activities Most Alluring to Me	Motivation	Deeper Motivation (Basic Human Need)

    b) For each of these activities, determine in the second column the underlying motivation that makes this activity so appealing to you. For example, if the activity is "Checking Facebook," the motivation might be "Seeing what my friends have been up to." If the activity is checking email, the motivation might be "Making sure everything is OK" or "Staying on top of my work."

c) In the third column, try to name *the basic human need* underlying the motivation you identified in the second column. For example, if the motivation in the second column is "Seeing what my friends have been up to," the deeper underlying motivation may be "Emotional connection." If the motivation in the second column is "Staying on top of my work," the deeper motivation may be "Be acknowledged for my competence" or "Make a contribution to society."

d) Write down more online activities with associated motivations and deeper underlying motivations. For example, if the online activity is "Make money," the motivation might be "Buy a new car" and the deeper underlying motivation may be "Approval," or "Acceptance," or even "Love." (Your implicit mental script may be "Someone will love me if I have money and a new car.")

The importance of this exercise is that you may have multiple motivations for any single activity, and understanding your rawest, most fundamental human needs associated with any activity you repeatedly engage in online will help you wrest yourself from its control. The more you can identify your own unmet human needs—those that impel you to repeatedly engage in any online activity in the hopes that you can meet them—the more you will reduce the power of this activity over you.

e) Acknowledge how well your online activities meet the basic human needs you have identified: in other words, assess the extent to which your online activities *actually* satisfy the basic human needs you are attempting to meet by engaging in them.

f) Based on what you have written in Steps (a) through (e), design some healthier, offline, real-time strategies to meet the basic human needs that impel you to go online. If you desire, apply what you write here to your **Action Plan** that you develop in the final section of the workbook.

INNER
LEADERSHIP
PRESS

Bringing It Home: Connecting with My Goals and Values

8) What are the most important lessons you've learned in this chapter that will influence how you use your phone/devices?

9) Based on these lessons, what new goals could you commit to? (Refer back to these goals in the final section of the workbook when you develop your Action Plan.)

10) How do these new goals reflect your values? What values do you stand for and want to be remembered for that are consistent with these new goals? (Refer back to these values in the final section of the workbook when you develop your Vision Statement.)

Notes on How I Will Reclaim My Freedom
and Happiness in the Digital Age

3

Social Information versus Social Connection

1) Do you find seeking social information appealing? If so, how does it benefit you? What does it enable? Describe a time when you sought social information.

2) Consider:

> *The Internet may be the most pandemic game of bait-and-switch we've ever collectively experienced as a society. It initially baited us with social information, then pulled a switch by promising us social connection. Yet ninety-nine times out of a hundred, it only delivers social information. It paradoxically tantalizes us into downgrading face-to-face interactions in anticipation of social connection, which remains perpetually elusive.*
>
> *This bait-and-switch is problematic, as social connection is widely considered one of the most important ingredients of happiness. It is for this reason, among others, that we relentlessly pursue meaningful relationships with others. Yet what the Internet provides—social information—does not increase happiness, as evidenced by an experimental study that found quitting Facebook causes an increase in well-being.*

Think back to a time when you went online seeking social connection and instead received only social information. How did it make you feel? How is this distinction important to how you approach your career and life?

INNER LEADERSHIP PRESS

3) Consider:

> *The television, typewriter, and telephone also accelerated other addictions. They offered new opportunities we never could have fathomed before their emergence, such as being entertained by people all over the world and receiving video imagery of current news events (the TV) and talking with just about anyone, anytime, no matter where in the world they might be (the telephone).*
>
> *The Internet is different from these previous inventions in two very critical ways. First of all, whether in desktop, laptop, tablet, or smart- phone form*—the Internet is all of the above inventions wrapped up in one unbelievably addic- tion-accelerating little package. *It's a one-stop shop. An all-in-one. It places you one click away from accessing, for the most part, every single communication invention that preceded it.*

Have you found any strategies to be effective in managing this new titan of all "connecting" technologies—the Internet—so it doesn't take over your life? What has worked for you?

4) Describe a time when the amount of time you spent on your phone/devices influenced your enjoyment of face-to-face interactions.

5) In which ways do you check social media to gather social information and compare yourself with others? How does this make you feel? Have you found any remedies for it?

INNER
LEADERSHIP
PRESS

6) Do you text and drive, despite knowing its dangers? Design a strategy to preempt texting and driving.

7) Consider the harmful aspects of being unable to control your use of the Internet in your life. How is this lack of control harmful to yourself and/or others? What can you do about it?

8) Do you use your phone while driving or in transit (such as when walking or taking public transportation)? What is the effect of this phone time on the level of stress you experience during the day?

9) Consider:

> *We have to make a quality-quantity distinction. How? By asking ourselves if an "always on" schedule—in which even "in-between time" (e.g., time spent walking, driving, or taking a bus, metro, or taxi to or from meetings or other work activities) is allocated to work or social activities—will net us the minimum amount of self-time necessary to be truly engaged and present with others once we step back onto the grid.*

Design a strategy to "let in-between time be in-between time." How can you better honor your desire for connection without engaging in addictive tendencies during your brief moments of "free" time during the day?

Bringing It Home: Connecting with My Goals and Values

10) What are the most important lessons you've learned in this chapter that will influence how you use your phone/devices?

11) Based on these lessons, what new goals could you commit to? (Refer back to these goals in the final section of the workbook when you develop your Action Plan.)

12) How do these new goals reflect your values? What values do you stand for and want to be remembered for that are consistent with these new goals? (Refer back to these values in the final section of the workbook when you develop your Vision Statement.)

INNER LEADERSHIP PRESS

Notes on How I Will Reclaim My Freedom
and Happiness in the Digital Age

4

The Brogrammer Brigade

1) Consider:

> Dopamine is not only released when you are pursuing a cognitive goal, such as finding a good travel deal. It is also released when you are pursuing an emotion-laden goal, such as trying to find the right partner. Electrochemical studies in male rats reveal that more dopamine is released in the presence of a female receptive rat than during actual copulation. In other words, dopamine is associated with the chase, not the catch.
>
> If you've ever spent more time on Netflix searching for a film than actually watching it, you are no stranger to this phenomenon. It's the feeling that we are progressing toward a goal, rather than actually enjoying the attainment of the goal, that releases dopamine.

What kinds of activities stimulate dopamine within you? What kinds of information keep you reaching for your phone, such that you end up touching it (if you are near the average) over 2,500 times daily? Describe how this process emerges within you.

2) What happens when you over-release dopamine? How does releasing too much dopamine influence your behavior vis-à-vis your phone/devices?

3) Consider:

> *Whether we survive or even thrive in the third millennium may depend on whether the goals we pursue online, spurred on by dopamine, are actually important. Are they?*

What goals do you pursue online? How important are they to you?

4) Consider:

> *Developmental milestones for babies emphasize "serve-and-return" interactions in which parents respond to moments when babies seek connection and assurance by smiling, making eye contact, and talking with them, which lays the foundation for babies' brains ... Women used to carry out the vital responsibility of facilitating the serve-and-return conversational duets that buffer the psychological and social complexities of growing up in an anxiety-filled world from which new life thrives. When women entered the workplace en masse ... no one filled in for them to carry out this critical role. No one except the screens, and they clearly don't do a very good job.*

Did your parents raise you with a "conversational duet"? How did their parenting style affect you?

INNER
LEADERSHIP
PRESS

5) If you have (or plan to have) children, how are you raising (will you raise) them vis-à-vis the electronic babysitter? If you do not have or plan to have children, how can you mentor the children of others? Design some strategies to raise your children or help raise other children rather than permitting them to be raised by screens.

6) In this example, consider the techniques in the brogrammers' arsenal to coopt your greatest asset in the current economy: your attention.

a) What are the techniques employed by the brogrammers to ensnare your attention such that you touch your phone, on average, over 2,500 times daily? Make a list of these techniques in the first column of the following table.

Successful Brogrammer Techniques to Capture My Attention	My Human Need That the Technique Capitalizes On	Strategy to Circumvent the Technique and Reclaim My Attention

 INNER LEADERSHIP PRESS

b) In the second column, describe your human need that the technique capitalizes on (e.g., my need for recognition, my need for belonging).

c) In the third column, design strategies to circumvent these techniques and recapture your own attention.

d) If you desire, integrate some of the strategies you've developed into your **Action Plan** in the final section of the workbook.

7) Consider:

> *Aside from the worthiness of each message, you can use the dopamine-inducing effects of email to your advantage … How? By checking email after lunch when you're tired and about to hit a lull. That way you can avoid artificial stimulants like sugar or soda or coffee. And the dopamine-releasing effects of seeking the empty inbox will wake you up.*

How can you leverage dopamine to your advantage, such as in the above example? Given your unique motivations and schedule, can you design a strategy to achieve this objective?

Bringing It Home: Connecting with My Goals and Values

8) What are the most important lessons you've learned in this chapter that will influence how you use your phone/devices?

9) Based on these lessons, what new goals could you commit to? (Refer back to these goals in the final section of the workbook when you develop your Action Plan.)

10) How do these new goals reflect your values? What values do you stand for and want to be remembered for that are consistent with these new goals? (Refer back to these values in the final section of the workbook when you develop your Vision Statement.)

Notes on How I Will Reclaim My Freedom and Happiness in the Digital Age

5

You Are the Crash Test Dummy

1) Consider:

> We can't point to Joe, who at age seventy has sat hunched over behind a screen for fifty years, and say, "Look at Joe's posture—he still stands and walks so well." We are the first screen-obsessed generation, and most of us haven't even made it through our third decade of everyday screen usage. So the jury is still out on the physical effects of protracted screen use.
>
> Ditto for the social, psychological, emotional, and spiritual effects. At age seventy, can Joe still effectively listen to others? Can he read emotions and nonverbal cues on others' faces? Does he still even feel empathy? Can he still adequately express himself to others in face-to-face conversations? Does he still have friends whom he's invested enough time and energy in over the years that they call sometimes and even visit once in a while?
>
> There is no Joe, so we cannot yet know the answer to this question.
>
> In other words, each of us is a digital Lucy (the name given to one of our earliest bipedal ancestors, 40 percent of whose skeleton was found in Ethiopia in 1974 by archeologists fond of loudly playing the Beatles' "Lucy in the Sky with Diamonds" each evening at their expedition camp). We are each a digital crash test dummy. We are the predecessors, and will become the ancestors, of a future generation of the human race that will have fully adapted to a digitally mediated environment.

In what way can each of us be considered a crash test dummy or a "Digital Lucy" when it comes to the effects of the Internet?

2) Have you noticed the effects of too much sitting on your body? How does it affect you physically?

INNER
LEADERSHIP
PRESS

3) Do you agree that "sitting is the new smoking"? Why or why not?

4) How many hours do you sit each day? Could you adjust your schedule to sit less? How?

5) What is your attitude toward retiring? How does it influence how you go about your current life? Consider a few strategies that could help you develop a healthier attitude toward retiring.

6) Consider:

> *After the car was invented, people sought any excuse to go for a drive. It was all the rage to go to drive-in theaters. After a while, people decided they really didn't need to sit in their cars while watching a movie. As the novelty of driving a car subsided, drive-in theaters faded into obscurity.*
>
> *A few decades later, in the late 1950s, another new technology, the television, was so captivating that it was moved from the living room into the dining room so families could watch their favorite shows during dinner. This practice was soon deemed uncouth and TVs were moved back to the living room. Perhaps we are currently experiencing a similar pendulum swing of a new technology.*

Do you think your overuse of technology is a response to "the new technology adoption pendulum"? Why or why not?

7) For this exercise, consider how to consume the best of the Internet without being consumed by it.

a) Consider:

> Thirty years ago, we never would have imagined we could see a video on just about anything we want, be in contact with people from all over the globe, think of a book we want to read or a song we want to hear and then—within seconds— read or listen to it. We would have been incredulous were we told that one day we would throw away our encyclopedias and have all the same information they once contained—at our fingertips 24-7, more easily accessible, at no apparent cost whatsoever.
>
> The Internet is so amazing, in fact, that we have each become like a kid who has taken up permanent residence in a candy store. We just can't get enough. My fear is that a whole generation of people will miss out on real life because they can never quench their voracious hunger to consume from the digital trough.

b) What are the benefits of the Internet in your life? List some of the most important benefits to you available online.

INNER
LEADERSHIP
PRESS

c) How is the Internet preventing you from experiencing "real life"? Can you design some strategies to reap the Internet's benefits and also make the most of the limited time you have left on this planet?

d) How much time would you like to allocate each day to capturing these benefits? At what times of the day?

e) If you desire, integrate some of the strategies you've developed into your **Action Plan** in the final section of the workbook.

8) Consider:

> *Fear of Missing Out (on social information, by being offline) becomes Actually Missing Out (on social connection, by being online). The FOMO/AMO irony points to an unsettling truth:* We may need to sub-optimize our Internet use in the short term in order to optimize our values, friendships, and well-being in the long term.

How does the FOMO/AMO irony play out in your life? What can you do about it? In addition to the Internet, what else may you need to sub-optimize in order to optimize what you value in the long term?

INNER
LEADERSHIP
PRESS

9) Consider BJ Fogg's story:

> *"I'm out surfing like I do every morning and I come in and there are my parents in their eighties, they're sitting there in my living room," the Stanford social scientist B. J. Fogg, who lives half the year on Maui, shared with me. "I walk in and they are on their phone and iPad. I say, 'Hi, I'm back' and they keep looking at their technology. They don't even look up at me. And I thought, 'You've got to be kidding me.' I come in, I see them first thing in the morning … I haven't seen them at Christmas, I haven't seen them at Thanksgiving and they're just so glued to their screen."*

Describe a time when you felt shut out by another person's screen staring. In which situations do you think others may have felt this way by your own screen staring? What can you do to change this behavior?

Bringing It Home: Connecting with My Goals and Values

10) What are the most important lessons you've learned in this chapter that will influence how you use your phone/devices?

11) Based on these lessons, what new goals could you commit to? (Refer back to these goals in the final section of the workbook when you develop your Action Plan.)

12) How do these new goals reflect your values? What values do you stand for and want to be remembered for that are consistent with these new goals? (Refer back to these values in the final section of the workbook when you develop your Vision Statement.)

INNER
LEADERSHIP
PRESS

Notes on How I Will Reclaim My Freedom and Happiness in the Digital Age

6

Your Digital Identity

1) What is your digital identity? How does it influence how you approach your career and life?

2) Which of the digital identities outlined in *Screened In* have you embodied at different times in your life? What appealed to you about each identity? How did each identity affect your life?

INNER
LEADERSHIP
PRESS

3) Consider:

Digital Native = *A person born after the advent of the Internet. Digital Natives typically do not question technology and face few, if any, existential issues related to its use. Many have been using Google and YouTube for longer than they have known how to read or write. The smartphone or iPad has become the toy of choice for many toddlers. A friend's daughter knew how to find the icon for Google on his smartphone, then the tab for YouTube, and then the icon for her favorite cartoon before reaching her second birthday. The third word learned by another friend's two-year-old son was "iPad." At three years old, our son learned how to use Google Voice to bring up any image he wanted and soon became fascinated with pictures of the solar system.*

Digital Settler = *A person born before the advent of the Internet. Many Digital Settlers, like myself, experience existential angst and are generally unsettled about the role of technology in their lives. They remember the way things were. They wax nostalgic about the analog life. Many once owned record players and miss the richer, deeper sound of albums. Most have left their old way of living behind, yet relish memories of the unmediated life. Some look back, some don't. Many vividly remember and have internalized a history of struggling with the Internet and mobile phones: waiting until 9 p.m. or the weekend to make cell phone calls or pay over a dollar per minute; listening to a sound not unlike a radio without an antenna indicating that their dial-up modem was connecting and usurping their land line and that the emails in their outbox would now send and the messages they'd been patiently waiting for would arrive in their inbox. They resent Digital Natives for having it so easy. In about eighty years there will be no more Digital Settlers left; we will all be Digital Natives.*

Are you a Digital Native or a Digital Settler? How does this identity influence how you've approached your phone/devices?

4) Consider:

> *A former writer of theater screenplays, Stanley Milgram inventively choreographed an experiment in which participants were ordered by an austere researcher in a lab coat to administer increasingly dangerous electric shocks to a man (a confederate in the experiment, meaning a person hired by Milgram) sitting in an adjacent room attempting to learn a series of words...Milgram's experiments shocked the world (no pun intended) when* 65 percent of participants continued administering the shocks to the full, 450-volt level...*When the victim of the electric shock was placed in close proximity to the participant, the percentage of participants willing to deliver shocks up to the maximum 450 volts dropped by over 50 percent.*

Reflect on the effects of co-presence as the only mechanism (in Milgram's experiment) to induce empathy and compassion and, ultimately, to reduce participants' willingness to deliver shocks to the other person. How can you integrate more co-presence into your life to induce more empathy and compassion toward others? (Consider integrating your response into your **Vision Statement** in the final section of the workbook.)

5) Consider:

> *The younger generation tends to possess a less solid sense of self as they are in the throes of puberty, adolescence, and growing up—a time when, almost by definition, they are focused on developing their personal identity. Older folks have had more time to build their skills in the complex task of self-regulation: they've simply had more practice at it.*
>
> *For this reason, psychological research has found that people become less moody and prone to experiencing negative emotions as adults, at least through their late middle age. They also become more comfortable with themselves, responsible, caring, and emotionally stable. In personality psychology, this phenomenon has been referred to as the "maturity principle."*

Think about your own current life stage and how you've developed over the course of your life. In what way has your ability to self-regulate improved? How does this ability influence how you use your phone/devices?

INNER
LEADERSHIP
PRESS

6) Consider:

> *Self-regulation often involves a difficult choice between an emotion and a value: a decision to permit your actions to be determined by either a momentary impulse or a larger vision of what you know your life can become. Although this choice is always there, if you haven't grown up with a connection to deeper, life-affirming values—or with the necessary inner strength to brave extended periods of solitude and develop such values fostered by (but not requiring) secure relation- ships with loving, attentive parents—then the perception of such a decision may be faint: more likely, your emotion or impulse du jour will dictate your behavior.*

Reflect on your own life story. How did the way you grew up influence how you regulate your emotions? Given your unique life path, what can you do now to improve your self-regulation? Design a few strategies to achieve this objective.

7) Consider the situation where adults are distracted by their phones while their children are stranded without these digital comfort objects (that end up producing even more anxiety in the long term). Is this fair? If not, what can you do about this injustice?

8) Consider:

> *I thought about the restaurant in Radesky's study and the children escalating their bids for attention from their parents who were too busy on their phones to be present. Then I remembered a family we recently sat next to at a restaurant near our home. Both parents were on their phones for the entire meal. Their three children were each on a tablet. Once in a while, I watched their daughter put her tablet down, put her chin in her hands, look around the table sadly, and then pick the tablet back up.*
>
> *I wanted to shake the father and shout, "What's the matter with you?! This is your one chance, and you're blowing it. You'll never have this time with your kids again. You're squandering your inheritance, the most beautiful gift you'll ever receive in this life. If the transcendent reasons don't convince you, consider that the less time and energy you invest in them now, the less they'll invest in you later."*

In which ways are you "squandering your inheritance" as a human being? What can you do about it now?

Bringing It Home: Connecting with My Goals and Values

9) What are the most important lessons you've learned in this chapter that will influence how you use your phone/devices?

10) Based on these lessons, what new goals could you commit to? (Refer back to these goals in the final section of the workbook when you develop your Action Plan.)

11) How do these new goals reflect your values? What values do you stand for and want to be remembered for that are consistent with these new goals? (Refer back to these values in the final section of the workbook when you develop your Vision Statement.)

INNER
LEADERSHIP
PRESS

Notes on How I Will Reclaim My Freedom and Happiness in the Digital Age

7

The Kids Are Not Alright

1) This exercise is about the importance of satisfying your need to belong so you can live a healthy life.

a) Consider:

> I asked [the social psychologist Roy Baumeister] why social ostracism or rejection, which now comes fast and furious through electronic communication, so easily sends us into a tailspin.
>
> Baumeister's answer reminded me why his work has inspired my research on loneliness and disconnection. "It thwarts one of the most basic and powerful drives in the human mind," he shared. "We evolved with a strong need to belong, so that we connect with others. Rejection and ostracism mean that one has failed to satisfy that need."
>
> The importance of this need has not escaped others intent on damaging an individual. In traditional societies, social ostracism was often used as the most severe form of punishment. This effect is more pronounced in younger than older people, as the rapidly developing brains of younger people are more highly sensitized to detect social exclusion.
>
> It is perhaps for this reason that the Cigna study released in 2020 counterintuitively found that it's not the elderly, as most anticipate, who are the loneliest in US society, but children and teens. Almost eight of every ten Gen Zers (79 percent) and over seven in ten Millennials (71 percent) are now lonely, compared to half of Baby Boomers (50 percent). This finding is extremely disconcerting, not only because of the suffering of our youngest generations, but also because they gradually replace the oldest and become our new society.

INNER
LEADERSHIP
PRESS

b) Why are the youngest members of our society currently the loneliest?

c) Can you relate to the plight of young people struggling to fit in? Describe a time when you felt like you were playing a role in order to belong. Did it help you feel less lonely? Reflect on this time in your life.

d) What can you do to help young people struggling with these challenging feelings of loneliness? Design a few strategies to help both young people and yourself reclaim a sense of belonging in their/your lives.

e) If you desire, integrate some of these strategies into your **Action Plan** in the final section of the workbook.

2) Consider a time when you observed the effects of digital devices on children. Did you notice a gender difference? Have you attempted to intervene in such a situation? Design some strategies to approach similar situations in the future.

3) Take a moment to breathe and then think about this question. Have you ever been cyber-bullied? What did it feel like? Did it have any effects on your life later on? If so, what did it lead to?

4) Have you ever cyber-bullied someone else? If so, describe the event. What motivated you to do so? Knowing its toxic effects, how can you now work to prevent cyber-bullying in our society?

INNER
LEADERSHIP
PRESS

5) Consider the social plight of Maria, a twenty-something accounts manager:

> *If you were to ask me, "how many of your two hundred sixty-one Instagram followers do you still talk to on a monthly basis?" I would answer ten. That includes my two siblings, close friends, and a few coworkers. I have used social media to share my personal life and experiences with others—with people I no longer socialize with anymore. This habit has stuck around because I feel like I need social media to stay alive in the social world. It feels like I need these outlets to keep up with everyone else. I believe that due to the amount of time I spend on social media, I have experienced growing feelings of isolation.*

Do you relate to Maria's experience? If so, how?

6) Now consider Nancy's experience with email:

> *I would ALWAYS constantly check my work emails to see if my boss has messaged me or if I am missing any important information at work, even checking emails when I would wake up at 2 a.m. I did not know that my addiction to my work emails was that extreme. For some reason, having unread messages in my inbox gives me anxiety.*

And Elaine's experience with social media:

> *Eight months ago, my father died unexpectedly. Following his death, I felt separated from the rest of my social connections by my complicated feelings of grief. I seemed to become disconnected from a world where life had not stopped for everyone else, while I was stuck on the loss of someone with whom I had always had a difficult relationship. I felt isolated by my extreme emotions, which was further compounded by a desire for social support while feeling incapable of reaching out for help or human connection. Additionally, I felt overwhelmed by the presence of social media. While I tried to avoid social media websites, occasional visits left me discouraged, as everyone else appeared to be posting life events and experiences that were so much more fulfilling than my own.*

INNER
LEADERSHIP
PRESS

Reflect on Nancy's relationship with email and Maria's and Elaine's relationships with social media. Describe any parallels to how you interact with these technologies in your own life.

7) This exercise is about how you regulate your use of social media.

   a) Consider:

   Ask yourself how you would experience your life if you were to develop meaningful ways to provide yourself the daily reassurance you need rather than seek it from other people who are also camouflaging their deeper feelings of insecurity behind their screens. What would you be able to create if you stopped posting on social media in hope of gaining the approval of others?

   What would be possible in your life if you were to instead devote your creative energies to developing projects less for short-term recognition and more for long-term impact?

   b) In which ways does social media help you in your life?

   c) How does social media harm you?

INNER LEADERSHIP PRESS

d) What would be possible in your life if you could better regulate your use of social media?

e) Design some strategies to achieve this objective.

f) If you desire, apply what you write here to your **Action Plan** that you develop in the final section of the workbook.

8) Consider that the number one reported emotion on Facebook is envy. Write about a time when you felt envious while on social media. How does envy play a role in keeping you glued to social media? What can you do to change this dynamic?

Bringing It Home: Connecting with My Goals and Values

9) What are the most important lessons you've learned in this chapter that will influence how you use your phone/devices?

10) Based on these lessons, what new goals could you commit to? (Refer back to these goals in the final section of the workbook when you develop your Action Plan.)

11) How do these new goals reflect your values? What values do you stand for and want to be remembered for that are consistent with these new goals? (Refer back to these values in the final section of the workbook when you develop your Vision Statement.)

Notes on How I Will Reclaim My Freedom and Happiness in the Digital Age

8

Digital Drift

1) Consider:

> *Digital Drift is the greatest obstacle to focus today. It's what you experience when you plan to go online for ten minutes to research something and the next thing you know it's three hours later and you've been looking at a friend's spring break pictures and sneaking excessively long glances at the photos of their scantily clad friends, or checking five travel websites for the best deal on a trip you are not even sure you will take, or checking the status updates of people five concentric circles removed from your closest friends.*

Do you agree that Digital Drift is the greatest obstacle to focus today? Why or why not?

2) Think back to a time when you experienced Digital Drift. How can you gain more control of how you use your digital devices and use them more intentionally?

3) This exercise is about how you can access the Internet and then leave healthy and intact.

a) Consider:

Every time you make the decision to look at your phone or laptop, imagine you are on a shopping trip. There are two primary forms of shopping: the first, the shopping walkabout, is to go see as much of the merchandise as possible so you know what's on sale and have a full awareness of the plethora of purchasing options available. The second, the shopping incursion, is to know exactly what you want, go in, find it, buy it, leave, done.

If you take the simple step of reorienting your mind and viewing the Internet as it rightfully is—an unprecedentedly enormous, interactive digital shopping mall—and only enter for a rapid in-and-out shopping incursion during which you retain your focus on finding precisely what you're looking for and then leaving; if you can bypass the massive candy-colored distractions lining your path at every moment that the human brain has never been biologically prepared to bypass; if you can overcome the best efforts of tens of thousands of software developers who have created every minute facet of that virtual shopping mall to ensnare you and never allow you to find the exit door so you spend every last dime of your most valuable currency in life—your time—before you saunter out and ashamedly schlep your way home, less of a person than when you entered; if you can do that, you will have just availed yourself of the most ubiquitous flea market in history without allowing it to spit out whatever is left of your life.

b) How can you "avail yourself of the most ubiquitous flea market in history without allowing it to spit out whatever is left of your life"?

c) Design a few strategies to enable you to make shopping incursions into this ubiquitous flea market and emerge again rapidly, whole, and intact.

d) If you desire, integrate some of these strategies into your **Action Plan** in the final section of the workbook.

INNER
LEADERSHIP
PRESS

4) Consider this finding from the Princeton theology experiment:

> *When in a hurry, 90 percent of Princeton theology students were unwilling to help an ailing man on the street while on their way to give a talk about helping an ailing man on the street.*

Consider one way your daily actions are consistent with your values. How do your phone/devices help or hinder you in achieving this consistency?

5) Consider the Digital Drift Divide:

> *According to a recent Kaiser Family Foundation study of over two thousand children and teens ages eight to eighteen, in 1999 children and teenagers with parents who do not have a college degree spent sixteen minutes more per day exposed to media in various forms (e.g., social media, TV, other electronic gadgets) than those with parents with a college degree. In 2010, this difference had increased to an hour and a half.*
>
> *Worse still, in 2010 African American and Hispanic children spent almost four and a half more hours per day watching television and playing video games than white children…This widening time-wasting gap is largely attributed by the study authors to more-educated mothers and fathers monitoring their children's use of their digital devices more closely than less-educated parents. In poorer families, it is not uncommon for parents to be working more than one job and to have less time for child rearing. For this new latchkey generation, Facebook has become the go-to babysitter.*

What are the effects of the Digital Drift Divide on the lives of low-income people? Can you think of reasons why this discrimination happens?

INNER LEADERSHIP PRESS

6) As a conscientious individual, what can you do to help narrow the Digital Drift Divide? Design a few strategies to help achieve this objective.

7) Consider:

> *Writing down a concrete goal helps you stay focused on what you want to create. This skill—maintaining your focus on a specific objective—has never been more critical in the history of humankind. With the advent of email, Facebook, and smartphones, never before have we had so many options, and distractions, at our fingertips.*
>
> *The next time you are about to glance down at your phone, ask yourself, "Why am I choosing this action? What higher-order purpose am I pursuing?" Then ask yourself, "How else could I spend my time to better achieve this purpose?"*

Write down three goals you can refer to when you are feeling tempted by your phone/devices.

8) If you desire, integrate some of these strategies into your **Action Plan** in the final section of the workbook.

9) This exercise is about the importance of family and how to protect this part of your life in the Digital Age.

  a) Why are family dinners so important for long-term health?

  b) Did you grow up with at least three family dinners per week? Please describe.

c) What does family mean to you now?

d) How can you create your own "family" (however you define it) as a protective means to help all of its members (including you) better navigate this life, especially vis-à-vis the many toxic distractions it contains?

e) Consider integrating what you have written into your **Vision Statement** in the final section of the workbook.

INNER
LEADERSHIP
PRESS

10) Were you raised by the electronic babysitter? What did it feel like? What did it lead to in your life?

11) If you have children, do you use the electronic babysitter? Why do you make this choice? What can you can do about it?

12) What strategies can you design to reduce the presence of the electronic babysitter in your life and the lives of the people you love?

13) If you desire, integrate some of these strategies into your **Action Plan** in the final section of the workbook.

Bringing It Home: Connecting with My Goals and Values

14) What are the most important lessons you've learned in this chapter that will influence how you use your phone/devices?

15) Based on these lessons, what new goals could you commit to? (Refer back to these goals in the final section of the workbook when you develop your Action Plan.)

16) How do these new goals reflect your values? What values do you stand for and want to be remembered for that are consistent with these new goals? (Refer back to these values in the final section of the workbook when you develop your Vision Statement.)

Notes on How I Will Reclaim My Freedom
and Happiness in the Digital Age

PART TWO:

THE NEW WORLD ORDER

9

The Meta-Democratization

1) This exercise is about the importance of slowing down to the natural speed of life.

   a) Cleary, technology has rapidly accelerated our lives. How has it done so in your life?

   b) What do you think about these words?

   If you want to achieve your most important goals
   as quickly as possible, slow down.

c) What are some effective strategies for slowing down your life?

d) If you desire, integrate some of these strategies into your **Action Plan** in the final section of the workbook.

2) Consider:

> *The researcher who developed the technical infrastructure of the Internet in the 1970s intended for it to be "not controlled by any group." Vint Cerf recently expressed his regret that the "Internet has become the opposite of what it was intended to be."*

Do you agree with Cerf? Why or why not?

3) Consider:

> *The critical question today is whether you can take the best that technology has to offer to improve your life without overdoing it and losing your humanity in the process. Each and every day of (what remains of) your life, you have the choice to spend it perched in front of a screen or interacting with nature and the real people you care about.*

How do you make this choice repeatedly throughout the day? How do you transform technology-induced automatic behavior into conscious behavior? Can you design a new strategy to help yourself better make this transformation?

Bringing It Home: Connecting with My Goals and Values

4) What are the most important lessons you've learned in this chapter that will influence how you use your phone/devices?

5) Based on these lessons, what new goals could you commit to? (Refer back to these goals in the final section of the workbook when you develop your Action Plan.)

6) How do these new goals reflect your values? What values do you stand for and want to be remembered for that are consistent with these new goals? (Refer back to these values in the final section of the workbook when you develop your Vision Statement.)

INNER
LEADERSHIP
PRESS

Notes on How I Will Reclaim My Freedom and Happiness in the Digital Age

10

The Brand Is You

1) Consider:

> *Our inexorable drive to create a personal brand causes us to become disconnected from who we really are. We think we are innocuously checking social media, but in fact we are nervously checking to see if our status has grown or is under attack, as nothing is more feared in the digital age than a threat to our personal brand.*
>
> *We live in a perpetual state of fear: we create a personal brand, attach our self-worth to its success, and then fear its loss—fear is always associated with loss—and desperately search for reassurance, every time we log on, that we are not losing our brand.*

What is your "personal brand"? How does it influence your online behavior?

2) Consider how the development and protection of a "personal brand" may induce compulsive Internet-fueled behavior. Have you noticed this occurrence in your own life? If so, how has it affected you?

3) Do you wish to change your behavior related to developing and protecting your "personal brand" online? What strategies would help you to do so?

4) Consider this Umberto Eco quote:

> *The Internet is one thing and its opposite. It could remedy the loneliness of many, but it turns out it has multiplied it; the Internet has allowed many to work from home, and that has increased their isolation. And it generates its own remedies to eliminate this isolation, Twitter, Facebook, which end up increasing it.*

How do the Italian novelist's words relate to your life? What can you do about it?

INNER
LEADERSHIP
PRESS

Bringing It Home: Connecting with My Goals and Values

5) What are the most important lessons you've learned in this chapter that will influence how you use your phone/devices?

6) Based on these lessons, what new goals could you commit to? (Refer back to these goals in the final section of the workbook when you develop your Action Plan.)

7) How do these new goals reflect your values? What values do you stand for and want to be remembered for that are consistent with these new goals? (Refer back to these values in the final section of the workbook when you develop your Vision Statement.)

Notes on How I Will Reclaim My Freedom and Happiness in the Digital Age

11

Convenience over Enjoyment

1) This exercise is about the importance of not sacrificing enjoyment or quality for convenience.

    a) Consider this example of the many decisions we make every day between convenience and enjoyment:

> *If you enjoy going to the supermarket and touching, smelling, feeling, seeing the food your family is going to consume and conversing with the checkout person and even sometimes other shoppers, you can decide to forego online supermarkets, where you often receive food closer to the expiration date anyway. If you enjoy going out with friends and socializing, you can stop engaging in laconic text exchanges and instead call a friend or two, go out, and leave the evening to chance.*

    b) When do you prioritize convenience over enjoyment or quality in your life?

c) When do you prioritize enjoyment or quality over convenience in your life?

d) Use the following table to identify instances in the various dimensions of your life where you prioritize convenience or enjoyment/quality.

Dimensions of My Life	Prioritize Convenience over Enjoyment/Quality	Prioritize Enjoyment/ Quality over Convenience
Family		
Friends		
Time with Self		
Career		
Intimate Relationship/ Dating		
Music		
Exercise		
Spirituality		
Eating		
Sleeping		

e) Consider the priorities you have identified in the above table. How do these priorities influence your online and offline behaviors?

f) Is there anything you would like to change about these priorities?

g) How can you better find a balance between short-term convenience and long-term enjoyment or quality in your life? What strategies could help you find this balance?

h) If you desire, apply what you write here to your **Action Plan** in the final section of the workbook.

2) This exercise emphasizes the importance of being fully present with the people you love and care about.

a) Consider this story from Chapter 6 of *Screened In*:

> One of my favorite stories, which I heard from meditation practitioner Tara Brach, is of a stockbroker who comes home one night at half past eight. He's talking on his smartphone trying to close a large deal. His eight-year-old daughter has been waiting for him to come home all day so she can tell him about something she learned in show-and-tell that day.
>
> When he enters the house she screams, "Daddy, Daddy, I want to show you something!"
> He says, "Not now, I'm on the phone."
> She knows her bedtime is nine, so she keeps jumping around him because she knows she won't be able to go to sleep unless she is able to talk with him. At eight forty-five, he's still busily talking on the phone.
> She starts tugging on his trousers, saying, "Daddy, Daddy, it'll just take a few minutes."
> Finally, he looks down at her and says, "What are you doing down there?"
> She replies, "I live down here, Daddy."

INNER
LEADERSHIP
PRESS

b) Reflect on when you have felt like this daughter. What did it feel like?

c) Take a moment to breathe. Now reflect on when you have acted like this father. What did it feel like?

d) How can you be more present with others in your life? What would be possible in your life if you were to do so?

e) Design some strategies to be where you are when you are and not somewhere else.

3) If you desire, integrate some of these strategies into your **Action Plan** in the final section of the workbook.

Bringing It Home: Connecting with My Goals and Values

4) What are the most important lessons you've learned in this chapter that will influence how you use your phone/devices?

5) Based on these lessons, what new goals could you commit to? (Refer back to these goals in the final section of the workbook when you develop your Action Plan.)

6) How do these new goals reflect your values? What values do you stand for and want to be remembered for that are consistent with these new goals? (Refer back to these values in the final section of the workbook when you develop your Vision Statement.)

INNER LEADERSHIP PRESS

Notes on How I Will Reclaim My Freedom
and Happiness in the Digital Age

12

Your Netflix Time

1) Where does your Netflix Time go? What do you do with the extra time technology affords you? Spend more time on your screens? Alternatively, do you engage in other offline, real-world pursuits? How do you feel about how you spend your Netflix Time?

2) Develop a few strategies to better use your Netflix Time.

3) This exercise is about convenience versus connection.

a) Consider how Keith Richards and Mick Jagger hit it off (offline) and launched the Rolling Stones. Recall a few recent times in your life when you had to make a choice between convenience or connection. What did you do?

b) Develop a few strategies to help you prioritize connection over convenience from here on out.

c) Check in with yourself in a week. How have you done?

d) If you desire, integrate some of these strategies into your **Action Plan** in the final section of the workbook.

4) Consider:

> *Our drive as a society toward convenience—facilitated by the intelligent, often mind-rather-than-heart-driven men who compete with each other for who can create the most efficient apps and websites—is relegating enjoyment to a nostalgic fantasy.*

Do you think we are becoming more mind- rather than heart-driven in the Digital Age? Why? If so, design a few strategies to return your heart to pole position.

5) Consider:

> *Consider the activities you engage in daily. Make a commitment to spend less time doing them alone and more time doing them outside of the house and in the company of others. As much as possible, try to leave your phone at home or at least in your car or locker during these potential opportunities for social interaction.*

Can you make this commitment? If so, keep a journal for the next week. Have you managed to spend more time outside with others? How has it felt? What has it led to in your life?

INNER
LEADERSHIP
PRESS

6) How can you adjust your work expectations so you are not online all day long? If you spend more time online during the work day than you would like, how you can healthily disengage when at home?

7) For you, is social connection "nice to do" or "need to do"? How does this distinction influence your everyday choices?

Bringing It Home: Connecting with My Goals and Values

8) What are the most important lessons you've learned in this chapter that will influence how you use your phone/devices?

9) Based on these lessons, what new goals could you commit to? (Refer back to these goals in the final section of the workbook when you develop your Action Plan.)

10) How do these new goals reflect your values? What values do you stand for and want to be remembered for that are consistent with these new goals? (Refer back to these values in the final section of the workbook when you develop your Vision Statement.)

Notes on How I Will Reclaim My Freedom and Happiness in the Digital Age

13

So Much Information, So Little Wisdom

1) Consider the message in this chapter that "Too much information is no information." Do you believe this to be true? Why or why not? If so, how does it play out in your life?

INNER
LEADERSHIP
PRESS

2) Consider:

> *Inside our phones, tablets, and laptops reside today's foxes: thousands of brogrammers whose job is to keep you there for as long as humanly possible, engaged in activities most of which hold very little importance to you in the long term. Tristan Harris (the former student of B. J. Fogg referred to earlier) once remarked, "You could say that it's my responsibility to exert self-control when it comes to digital usage, but that's not acknowledging that there's a thousand people on the other side of the screen whose job is to break down whatever responsibility I can maintain."*
>
> *In many ways, this book is about how to exercise our responsibility in the face of these unprecedented technological distractions and wrest our attention back from the brogrammers.*

List three apps that keep you staring at your screen. Design one strategy for each that will help you reclaim the attention the brogrammers have wrested away from you.

3) Consider a statement from this chapter: "Most social media is neither." What does this mean? Do you find it to be true? Why or why not? Develop a strategy to better regulate your use of social media.

4) Consider Monica's experience at dinner with friends:

> *I've been reflecting on this experience. It has made me aware of how much we are on our phones, but not really talking. My husband and I went out to dinner with another couple, and it was incredible that most of the time they were on their phones. My friend posted on Facebook, "Having a great time catching up with great friends." But she was on her Instagram most of the night. We really weren't connecting or having a real conversation. I felt like calling them out, like why was I even there? They made me feel unimportant since they couldn't even hold a conversation because they were distracted by their smartphones. But they were not the only ones, as I looked up and around the restaurant, I saw a sea of people with their faces buried in their phones.*

Write about a time when you had a similar experience. How did it make you feel?

5) If Monica's experience is increasingly the norm, what can you do about it? Design a few strategies to change this norm in your own life.

6) How many close friends do you have with whom you can talk about important issues? Are you content with the robustness and meaningfulness of your social life? If not, what would you like to do to change it?

7) Consider integrating what you write into your **Vision Statement** in the final section of the workbook.

Bringing It Home: Connecting with My Goals and Values

8) What are the most important lessons you've learned in this chapter that will influence how you use your phone/devices?

9) Based on these lessons, what new goals could you commit to? (Refer back to these goals in the final section of the workbook when you develop your Action Plan.)

10) How do these new goals reflect your values? What values do you stand for and want to be remembered for that are consistent with these new goals? (Refer back to these values in the final section of the workbook when you develop your Vision Statement.)

INNER
LEADERSHIP
PRESS

Notes on How I Will Reclaim My Freedom
and Happiness in the Digital Age

INNER
LEADERSHIP
PRESS

PART THREE:

RECONNECTED

14

Direct Your Use of Technology, Not the Other Way Around

1) This exercise is about aligning your life vision with your everyday actions.

a) Consider:

The critical challenge in the third millennium is the same as in the first: aligning your values with your behavior. What 90 percent of the Princeton theology students in the Good Samaritan study were unable to achieve. To first develop a vision for how you want to live your life and then live it daily.

To rise to this challenge, ask the best version of yourself—what we could call your higher self—a few questions, such as "How do you desire that I spend my time?", "How do you want me to act toward the people I care about?", and "For what do you want me to be remembered?"

Whatever emanates from this self-dialogue is how you should spend your time. If you can use your clever online tools to achieve some of your most important life goals, all power to you; I'll step out of your way right now. Yet every other moment you spend on your devices is as beneficial to your life as sitting in your car, turning on the ignition, and stepping on the pedal without a destination.

Every moment of every day you are making a decision about how to spend your time. If your goal is to have close friends to share your life with, determine how you will allocate your time to build those friendships. If you wish to spend more time in reality *and less time sitting behind a screen typing into a keypad* about reality, *take some time this week to design some strategies to limit your virtual time, such as a daily screen-time maximum.*

INNER
LEADERSHIP
PRESS

b) Write down three values or features that define your life vision. Now describe how your daily actions with respect to technology are either aligned or misaligned with that vision.

c) Design a few strategies to better align your daily actions. (You will learn more about how to align your life vision and daily actions in the final section of the workbook. Consider this exercise a test run.)

d) Share these strategies with a good friend. Ask your friend to also develop their own strategies to achieve the same objective.

e) Test out these strategies for the next week.

f) Report to your friend (and vice versa) on what works and what doesn't.

g) Based on your experience, redesign some of your strategies.

h) Go to (d).

INNER
LEADERSHIP
PRESS

2) Consider app programmers' use of color to manipulate you. Have you observed this in your life? If so, what can you do about it?

3) Are you willing to change your phone to grayscale? Why or why not? If so, report back on how this change is influencing your phone use.

Bringing It Home: Connecting with My Goals and Values

4) What are the most important lessons you've learned in this chapter that will influence how you use your phone/devices?

5) Based on these lessons, what new goals could you commit to? (Refer back to these goals in the final section of the workbook when you develop your Action Plan.)

6) How do these new goals reflect your values? What values do you stand for and want to be remembered for that are consistent with these new goals? (Refer back to these values in the final section of the workbook when you develop your Vision Statement.)

INNER
LEADERSHIP
PRESS

Notes on How I Will Reclaim My Freedom
and Happiness in the Digital Age

15

Downgrade Social Media, Upgrade Your Relationships

1) Reflect on the chapter title: "Downgrade Social Media, Upgrade Your Relationships." Then consider:

> *The only way to downgrade the value of social media in your life is to upgrade the value of authentic, real-time connections with the people you care about—or could care about if you took the time to get to know them better.*

How can you upgrade your real-time connections with the important people in your life? Design a few strategies to do so.

2) This exercise is about the link between over-using your phone/devices and loneliness.

    a) Consider:

> *Given the Cigna study released in 2020 that found that over 60 percent of Americans are lonely and the well-established link between high technology use and loneliness—a recent meta-analysis, for instance, found that lonely people spend more time on Facebook than non-lonely people—it is likely that most of the people who return your calls with a text or email are actually lonely. They have likely dug themselves into a digitally circumscribed hole, one small finger-tap- ping chunk of digital text at a time, from which they do not know how to exit.*

    b) Do you increase your screen use because you feel lonely? What does this behavior lead to in your life?

c) What other alternatives can you turn to when you feel lonely?

d) Design some strategies to reduce the power of the technology-loneliness link in your life.

3) This exercise is about how you manage the emotion of loneliness.

a) Consider:

Spending your days denying the loneliness you feel (e.g., suppression) when the people you used to count on no longer return your calls or stop by because they have become tethered to their phones is a recipe that will only create the conditions for your loneliness to compound and become less manageable. Instead, you can reengineer your thinking (i.e., cognitive reappraisal) about their social distancing and call it by a new name: their digitally induced atrophying of social abilities that's exacerbating not only your loneliness, but their own.

b) Why doesn't suppression work very well as an emotion regulation strategy?

c) Design a few strategies to cognitively reappraise and "reframe" your loneliness so it holds less power over you.

d) If you desire, integrate some of the strategies you've developed into your **Action Plan** in the final section of the workbook.

4) Do you call your parents or other people to whom you are close more because they are the only ones who will answer the phone? Who are the reliable people in your life whom you call because they will answer?

5) This exercise is about how to protect and sustain your "social gold." Consider:

> *Returning a text takes a few seconds and is a meager reciprocal social act; returning a call is a more significant investment in the relationship. Over time, the people who return and initiate calls, and collaborate to parlay those calls into in-person meetings, become the friends we need in the digital age.*
>
> *These people become our most coveted social resource, our social gold. The only ones who enables us to revitalize our social life. The only people standing between us and the formidable, ever-encircling tentacles of loneliness.*

a) Which of your friends are part of your "social gold": people who will either answer the phone or return your call promptly? List out your "social gold" in the first column—the people who most reciprocate your social overtures and desire a relationship with you.

My Social Gold	Social Responsiveness Rating

b) How does it feel to have these people in your life? Alternatively, how does it feel to not have many such people in your life?

c) In the second column, indicate how socially responsive these people are to you by giving them a rating between 1 (extremely unresponsive) and 10 (extremely responsive).

d) Design a few strategies to make the people who are a part of your "social gold"—the most responsive and present people in your life in the second column above—more of a priority in your life so you take them for granted less and appreciate and value them more.

e) Now design a few strategies to create more of these reliable relationships in your life and expand your "social gold."

f) If you desire, integrate some of these strategies into your **Action Plan** in the final section of the workbook.

6) This exercise is about the Communication Reciprocation Downgrade, a threat to developing and sustaining your "social gold." Consider:

> *The Communication Reciprocation Downgrade … occurs when you make a media-rich overture to someone (e.g., a phone call) and they offer a media-poor reply (e.g., a text or email).*

a) Consider the table you developed in the previous exercise. Who sometimes gives you the Communication Reciprocation Downgrade? How does it feel when they do that?

b) Do you wish to call these people less frequently? Develop a strategy to do so.

c) To whom do you sometimes give the Communication Reciprocation Downgrade? How do you think it feels for them?

d) Are there some people you give a Communication Reciprocation Downgrade to that you'd like to treat better? Design a strategy to do so.

e) Based on what you've written, consider developing either an entry in your **Vision Statement** or a goal in your **Action Plan** in the final section of the workbook.

7) Consider:

> *If you wish to reinvigorate your relationships, the question you have to answer is how you can circumvent the increasingly digitally mediated habits of others. Design some strategies to develop more meaningful connections with others—such as calling an old friend, or going on a group hike, or going sailing or fencing or to a local park and being friendly with the people you meet there—and then give them a try. In the process, remind yourself that new friends do not come along every day and you will have to try and try again to bring the kinds of people you desire into your life.*

Bring to mind a relationship that you would like to reinvigorate. Develop a strategy to help achieve this objective.

8) Design a few strategies to develop more meaningful relationships in your life.

INNER
LEADERSHIP
PRESS

Bringing It Home: Connecting with My Goals and Values

9) What are the most important lessons you've learned in this chapter that will influence how you use your phone/devices?

10) Based on these lessons, what new goals could you commit to? (Refer back to these goals in the final section of the workbook when you develop your Action Plan.)

11) How do these new goals reflect your values? What values do you stand for and want to be remembered for that are consistent with these new goals? (Refer back to these values in the final section of the workbook when you develop your Vision Statement.)

Notes on How I Will Reclaim My Freedom and Happiness in the Digital Age

16

Digital Limiting Strategies

1) This exercise is about strategies to limit your time online. Consider:

Here are a few Digital Limiting Strategies some of my clients and friends have successfully practiced:

- *A parent enforces "blackout periods" for their kids during which they are not allowed to access any digital technology.*
- *Meals are off limits (e.g., no smartphones). One client and his wife purposefully leave their phones in their bedroom when they have breakfast and dinner. This practice began when, on a few occasions, he asked her during dinner, "Did you see that email I sent you?" and she replied, "No, because my phone is upstairs. I'm not looking at it."*
- *One family has a basket next to the door to their dining room where phones are turned off and deposited before meals. Whether you leave your phone in your bedroom, the foyer, a basket, or a closet, the point is to leave it far enough away so you will not see or hear alerts or notifications and will hopefully be too lazy to retrieve it to punctuate (and, if done enough times, derail) a conversation about a fact check on Saturday's weather or the birthplace of Genghis Khan.*
- *Create and plan in advance distinct phone-free events with your family and friends. Obtain their buy-in early so they're psychologically ready for it when it happens.*
- *My favorite, which merits much more practice: when a group of friends goes out for a meal, the first person to check their phone pays the bill.*

a) Design some Digital Limiting Strategies.

b) Monitor how effective these Digital Limiting Strategies are over the next week.

c) Based on your experience, redesign your Digital Limiting Strategies as necessary.

d) If you desire, integrate some of these Digital Limiting Strategies into your **Action Plan** in the final section of the workbook.

2) Consider how the inability to go "cold turkey" keeps technology-mediated addictions strong. Design a few strategies to circumvent this dilemma and direct your use of technology rather than it directing you.

3) This exercise is derived from the Make It Happen exercise (in this chapter of *Screened In*):

a) Acknowledge how you spend your time online. In the first column, identify the specific online "projects" you embark on that seem to never have an end in sight and continually pique your acquisitive instinct, such as downloading music or movies, or researching potential partners to date, or emptying your inbox.

Online Uses of Time	Desired Weekly Maximum Time	Actual Weekly Maximum Time: Week 1	Actual Weekly Maximum Time: Week 2	Actual Weekly Maximum Time: Week 3

b) In the second column, give yourself a weekly maximum of time to dedicate to each of these activities. Select the amount of time depending on how this activity aligns with your deeper values and life vision.

c) Share these weekly maximums with a good friend (who ideally also does this exercise and shares their weekly maximums with you), perhaps in a spreadsheet. By transforming this exercise into a social commitment, you increase your chances of adhering to it as you and your friend hold each other accountable.

d) At the end of each week for the next three weeks, in the third column compare your actual hours spent on each of these activities with your desired weekly maximum. You and your friend can share your respective progress over lunch, while going on a walk together, or at a café.

e) If you surpass the limit, together with your friend, design strategies to reduce your hours. Alternatively, make adjustments to the weekly maximum if you deem it necessary.

INNER
LEADERSHIP
PRESS

Bringing It Home: Connecting with My Goals and Values

4) What are the most important lessons you've learned in this chapter that will influence how you use your phone/devices?

5) Based on these lessons, what new goals could you commit to? (Refer back to these goals in the final section of the workbook when you develop your Action Plan.)

6) How do these new goals reflect your values? What values do you stand for and want to be remembered for that are consistent with these new goals? (Refer back to these values in the final section of the workbook when you develop your Vision Statement.)

Notes on How I Will Reclaim My Freedom
and Happiness in the Digital Age

17

The Heart of Darkness

and

Contain Your Phone, Expand Your Life

1) This exercise is derived from the first Make It Happen exercise (in this chapter of *Screened In*):

    a) Turn off all notifications on your phone and, if you are willing to take a bold, courageous step to severely reduce the allure of your phone, set it to grayscale (see Chapter 14 of *Screened In* for why and how to perform this sacrilegious, countercultural transgression against Big Tech).

    b) Rate your apps in terms of how addictive they are. Which are the few apps you are always checking? Write down their names in the first column and their "addictiveness level" in the second column.

App Name	Addictiveness Level (Rating from 1 to 10 Where 10 Is Most Addictive)	New Maximum Number of Times I Will Check This App Each Day

c) Acknowledge how many times per day you are checking your text messages and other addictive apps (which may include email, WhatsApp, Snapchat, Bumble, Amazon, CNN or BBC, Zillow, or Facebook). Use this frequency to refine the "addictiveness levels" in the second column.

d) Envision what your life would be like if you were to check these apps much less often. Write a few sentences describing how your life would be different and how it would feel, including how often you would like to check each app if you were controlling your use of technology rather than technology (meaning the brogrammers who design it) controlling its use of you.

e) Write down the new maximum number of times you will check these apps daily in the final column.

f) Move your text messaging and other addictive apps to the inner station, the final screen on your smartphone, the farthest screen from your home screen that you have to swipe to the highest number of times, the Heart of Darkness—the heart of your addiction.

g) Check in with yourself daily about how you are doing in terms of only treading into the Heart of Darkness and checking those apps with the frequency you specified in Step (b). (Please feel free to check for individual text or email messages once in a while using the Side Door, but don't abuse this option.) Make a concerted effort to travel into and check the apps within the Heart of Darkness for messages quickly—usually for no more than a few minutes. Note the times of the day when you will use your limited access to your texting and other addictive final-screen apps.

INNER
LEADERSHIP
PRESS

h) Note how you feel, and how your experience of life is changing (as a number of my conference participants and I have done in the preceding pages) now that you travel into the Heart of Darkness much less frequently. Don't get down on yourself if you exceed your desired frequency on any particular day. That would reduce your self-esteem and be counterproductive. Instead, be honest with yourself about the basic human needs that induce you to open any particular app more than you would like. Then recommit to your goal of only checking that app the next day up to the maximum you identified in Step (b). (Alternatively, if you feel that your goal was too draconian, be more realistic and allow yourself to enter the Heart of Darkness one or a few more times daily. Create a goal that is "ambitious yet attainable.")

i) Periodically recalibrate. Every week or two, return to Step (a) and make updates if necessary.

j) If you desire, integrate some of these strategies into your **Action Plan** in the final section of the workbook.

2) This exercise is derived from the second Make It Happen exercise (in this chapter of *Screened In*):

a) Create a Heart of Darkness Journal: Write at least twice per week for the next seven weeks in your journal about how you are experiencing this change in how you use your phone. Use these questions as a (loose) guide to help you write about your experience (e.g., creatively free-flow write rather than answering these questions one after the other; like sleeping with ghosts, let the questions be a guideline, not a rule):

   i.   How does this practice feel for me?

   ii. Am I experiencing any changes in my life as a consequence of this practice?

   iii. Am I experiencing any changes (from when I first started) in terms of how I feel about this practice?

   iv. How (if at all) are my relationships changing as a result of this practice?

   v.   What (if anything) is this experience changing about how I view my phone and its role in my life?

   vi. After you complete the Heart of Darkness Challenge, go to Appendix A (in *Screened In*) and read a few sample Heart of Darkness Challenge Journals. Compare your own Heart of Darkness Challenge Journal to those in Appendix A and ask yourself what you have learned from this self-imposed social experiment. What will you do differently going forward based on what you've learned?

INNER
LEADERSHIP
PRESS

My Heart of Darkness Journal

Week 1 | Date: _____

Week 2 | Date: _____

My Heart of Darkness Journal

Week 3 | Date: _____

Week 4 | Date: _____

My Heart of Darkness Journal

Week 5 | Date: _____

Week 6 | Date: _____

My Heart of Darkness Journal

Week 7 | Date: _____

Week 8 | Date: _____

 INNER LEADERSHIP PRESS

Bringing It Home: Connecting with My Goals and Values

3) What are the most important lessons you've learned in this chapter that will influence how you use your phone/devices?

4) Based on these lessons, what new goals could you commit to? (Refer back to these goals in the final section of the workbook when you develop your Action Plan.)

5) How do these new goals reflect your values? What values do you stand for and want to be remembered for that are consistent with these new goals? (Refer back to these values in the final section of the workbook when you develop your Vision Statement.)

Notes on How I Will Reclaim My Freedom and Happiness in the Digital Age

INNER
LEADERSHIP
PRESS

Commencement

1) This exercise is about personal alignment.

  a) Consider:

> *I leave you to apply what you have learned in this book in your own life with the deep, heartfelt wish that you will discover the key to the digitally-3D-printed shackles that have ossified around your ankles, and, ultimately, your own path to achieve freedom from the technology that has ensnared us all. I would like to end with the powerful call to action by the rabbinic sage Hillel the Elder that has been adopted by many social activists:*

If not you, who? If not now, when?

  b) Design a few overarching strategies that encapsulate what you have learned in *Screened In* to live free in the Digital Age.

  c) If you desire, integrate some of these strategies into your **Action Plan** in the final section of the workbook.

d) For each strategy, identify an underlying value that is consistent with the strategy.

e) Consider integrating what you write into your **Vision Statement** in the final section of the workbook.

f) After one week, take stock of how you are implementing each strategy. Then consider the underlying values you identified and revise or renew your strategies.

How to Develop a Vision Statement and Action Plan

Vision without action is a daydream.
Action without vision is a nightmare.
—Ancient Japanese proverb

The exercises in this final section of the workbook will make much more of an impact in your life if you develop a Vision Statement and an Action Plan. Here is a brief summary of how to develop each.

Vision Statement:

A **Vision Statement** is a timeless statement of your core values and life vision.
Here are the characteristics of a Vision Statement:

- Timeless

- Unattainable (there will always be more to do to attain it)

- Statement of Core Values

- What you will always want to accomplish, but never will—a journey to a destination you will never reach

- Will always inspire hope

There is no better way to understand a new strategy than to consider how another person has applied it in their life. Here are a few entries from the Vision Statement of a good friend, Keith, an athletic director at a Florida university. Note each begins with the word "To," which indicates it is designed to move you *toward* a new destination in your life.

- To understand my student-athletes and acknowledge their accomplishments on a personal level

INNER
LEADERSHIP
PRESS

- To help my team members to grow in their professional development

- To encourage my coaches and athletes to become engaged in community service

- To develop and sustain a positive attitude about life. As an African-American I know there will be obstacles in life, and I must be positive when these obstacles present themselves and develop strategies to overcome them.

Action Plan:

An **Action Plan** is a time-sensitive statement of SMART goals (Specific, Measurable, Aligned with your Vision Statement, Realistic and Time-based) you plan to accomplish in the next year. An Action Plan is guided by Napoleon Hill's sage principle: "A goal is a dream with a deadline."

Here are the characteristics of an Action Plan:

- Time-sensitive

- Usually one-year time frame

- Concrete, smaller goals

Here are a few examples of SMART Action Plan goals for Keith that are aligned with his Vision Statement entry "To encourage my coaches and athletes to become engaged in community service." (Note: each Vision Statement entry can spawn multiple Action Plan goals.)

- Allocate $10,000 per year to incentives for my coaches and athletes to participate in community service.

- Preside over one meeting each quarter that each features at least 3 exemplary community-service initiatives of my coaches and athletes and how they are rewarded for their efforts.

Here are a few other examples of SMART Action Plan goals related to managing technology use:

- Check text messages and other apps on my phone at most three times daily (does not include the Side Door strategy).

- Complete two hours of creative work each morning before checking emails.

- Do not check emails after 6 p.m. or on the weekends.

Here is a summary of the differences between a **Vision Statement** and an **Action Plan**:

Vision Statement	Action Plan
Timeless	Time sensitive
Unattainable (there will always be more to do to attain it)	Attainable
Statement of core values; desired, idyllic image of the future	Statement of SMART goals

1) Write initial drafts of your **Vision Statement** and **Action Plan** below.

2) Read them each week and make revisions as necessary.

INNER
LEADERSHIP
PRESS

My Vision Statement

My Vision Statement

INNER
LEADERSHIP
PRESS

My Action Plan

My Action Plan

INNER
LEADERSHIP
PRESS

Acknowledgments

To my wife, Karla: thank you for your patience and support throughout these past ten years as I researched and wrote this book. Thank you also for inspiring me with an example of a mother dedicated to raising her children with steadfast connection in the digital age.

To my editors, Sheridan McCarthy and Stanton Nelson of Meadowlark Publishing Services: thank you for your integrity, patience, authenticity, and uncanny ability to catch even the minutest of errors. I am so grateful to have had the opportunity to learn from you.

To my cover designer, Mark Eimer, and layout designer, Diana Wade: you each were once again wonderful to work with. Thank you.

To my reviewers—Annie Acosta, Jeffrey Brudney, Emily McConnell, Kris Olsen, and Kate Perry: thank you for providing such thoughtful and detailed feedback on the manuscript. Your painstaking efforts have significantly improved the *Screened In Companion Workbook*.

To you, the reader: thank you for and enabling me to live my purpose of helping people experience and facilitate connection and create personal and social change.